GIVING THANKS TO GOD

Jesus Calling Bible Study Series

JESUS CALLING BIBLE STUDY SERIES

GIVING THANKS TO GOD

EIGHT SESSIONS

Sarah Young

with Karen Lee-Thorp

THOMAS NELSON
Since 1798

Published in Nashville, Tennessee, by Nelson Books, an imprint of Thomas Nelson. Nelson Books and Thomas Nelson are registered trademarks of HarperCollins Christian Publishing, Inc.

ISBN 978-0-310-08365-8

First Printing November 2016 / Printed in the United States of America

CONTENTS

INTRODUCTION

Sometimes our busy and difficult lives give us the impression that God is silent. We cry out to Him, but our feelings tell us that He isn't answering our prayers. In this, our feelings are incorrect. God hears the prayers of His children and speaks right into the situations in which we find ourselves. The trouble is that our lives are often too hectic, our minds too distracted, for us to take in what He offers.

This *Jesus Calling* Bible study is designed to help individuals and groups meditate on the words of Scripture and hear them not just as words said to people long ago but as words said to us today in the here and now. The goal is to help the heart open up and respond to what the mind reads—to encounter the living God as He speaks through the Scriptures. The writer to the Hebrews tells us:

> In the past God spoke to our ancestors through the prophets at many times and in various ways, but in these last days he has spoken to us by his Son, whom he appointed heir of all things, and through whom also he made the universe. The Son is the radiance of God's glory and the exact representation of his being, sustaining all things by his powerful word.
>
> —HEBREWS 1:1–3

God has spoken to us through His Son, Jesus Christ. The New Testament gives us the chance to walk with Jesus, see what He does, and hear Him speak into the sometimes confusing situations in which we find ourselves. The Old Testament tells us the story of how God prepared a people to be the family of Jesus, and in the experiences of those men and women we find our own lives mirrored.

THE GOAL OF THIS SERIES

The *Jesus Calling Bible Study Series* offers you a chance to lay down your cares, enter God's Presence, and hear Him speak through His Word. You will get to spend some time silently studying a passage of Scripture, and then, if you're meeting with a group, openly sharing your insights and hearing what others discovered. You'll also get to discuss excerpts from the *Jesus Calling* devotional that relate to the themes of the Bible passages. In this way, you will learn how to better make space in your life for the Spirit of God to speak to you through the Word of God and the people of God.

THE FLOW OF EACH SESSION

Each session of this study guide contains the following elements:

- CONSIDER IT. The two questions in this opening section serve as an icebreaker to help you start thinking about the theme of the session, connecting it to your own past or present experience and allowing you to get to know the others in your group more deeply. If you've had a busy day and your mind is full of distractions, these questions can help you better focus.

- EXPERIENCE IT. Here you will find two readings from *Jesus Calling* along with some questions for reflection. This is your chance to talk with others about the biblical principles found within the *Jesus Calling* devotions. Can you relate to what each reading describes? What insights from God's Word does it illuminate? What does it motivate you to do? This section will assist you in applying these biblical principles to your everyday habits.

- STUDY IT. Next you'll explore a Scripture passage connected to the session topic and the readings from *Jesus Calling*. You will not only analyze these Bible passages but also pray through them in ways designed to engage your heart and your head. You'll first talk with your group about what the verse or verses means and then spend several minutes in silence, letting God speak into your life through His Word.

- LIVE IT. Finally, you will find five days' worth of suggested Scripture passages that you can pray through on your own during the week. Suggested questions for additional study and reflection are provided.

FOR LEADERS

If you are leading a group through this study guide, please see the Leader's Notes at the end of the guide. You'll find background on the design of the study as well as suggested answers for some of the study questions.

GIVING THANKS FOR GOD'S ABUNDANCE

CONSIDER IT

Thankfulness is a skill we can develop with practice. It's just a matter of pausing and noticing the abundance with which God has filled our lives. We can choose to view life through the lens of deprivation (noticing everything we don't have and worrying that there is never enough for us) or through the lens of abundance (noticing everything we do have and trusting that a good God will provide for us). Which will we choose? In this session, we'll see what a difference it can make when we choose to view life through the lens of God's abundance.

1. *What is one thing for which you're thankful to God?*

Family

2. *How challenging would it be for you to come up with ten things for which you're thankful? Why do you think it's easy or hard for you?*

Easy — I feel God has blessed me in
so many ways

EXPERIENCE IT

"Bring Me the sacrifice of thanksgiving. Take nothing for granted, not even the rising of the sun. Before Satan tempted Eve in the Garden of Eden, thankfulness was as natural as breathing. Satan's temptation involved pointing Eve to the one thing that was forbidden her. The garden was filled with luscious, desirable fruits, but Eve focused on the one fruit she couldn't have rather than being thankful for the many good things freely available. This negative focus darkened her mind, and she succumbed to temptation.

"When you focus on what you don't have or on situations that displease you, your mind also becomes darkened. You take for granted life, salvation, sunshine, flowers, and countless other gifts from Me. You look for what is wrong and refuse to enjoy life until that is 'fixed.' When you approach Me with thanksgiving, the Light of My Presence pours into you, transforming you through and through. *Walk in the Light* with Me by practicing the discipline of thanksgiving."

—FROM *JESUS CALLING*, APRIL 6

3. *What was Eve's mistake when it came to being thankful?*

Focusing on what she didn't have

4. *What's wrong with focusing on what you don't have?*

You tend to forget all the good
things you've been given

"Let Me teach you thankfulness. Begin by acknowledging that everything—all your possessions and all that you are—belongs to Me. The dawning of each new day is a gift from Me, not to be taken for granted. The earth is vibrantly alive with My blessings, giving vivid testimony to My Presence. If you slow down your pace of life, you can find Me anywhere.

"Some of My most precious children have been laid aside in sickbeds or shut away in prisons. Others have voluntarily learned the discipline of spending time alone with Me. The secret of being thankful is learning to see everything from My perspective. My world is your classroom. *My Word is a lamp to your feet and a light for your path*."

—From *Jesus Calling*, April 29

5. *How does it foster thankfulness when you acknowledge that all you have and all you are belong to God?*

6. *Name one of the things you currently rely on to nurture your body or your soul. What do you think is God's perspective on this?*

Prayer - closer walk with the Lord.

STUDY IT

Read aloud the following passage from Genesis 2:8–9, 15–17, and 3:1–8. The woman in the story is Eve, the man is Adam, and the serpent is Satan.

²:⁸ Now the LORD God had planted a garden in the east, in Eden; and there he put the man he had formed. ⁹ The LORD God made all kinds of trees grow out of the ground—trees that were pleasing to the eye and good for food. In the middle of the garden were the tree of life and the tree of the knowledge of good and evil. . . .

¹⁵ The LORD God took the man and put him in the Garden of Eden to work it and take care of it. ¹⁶ And the LORD God commanded the man, "You are free to eat from any tree in the garden; ¹⁷ but you must not eat from the tree of the knowledge of good and evil, for when you eat from it you will certainly die." . . .

³:¹ Now the serpent was more crafty than any of the wild animals the LORD God had made. He said to the woman, "Did God really say, 'You must not eat from any tree in the garden'?"

² The woman said to the serpent, "We may eat fruit from the trees in the garden, ³ but God did say, 'You must not eat fruit from the tree that is in the middle of the garden, and you must not touch it, or you will die.'"

⁴ "You will not certainly die," the serpent said to the woman. ⁵ "For God knows that when you eat from it your eyes will be opened, and you will be like God, knowing good and evil."

⁶ When the woman saw that the fruit of the tree was good for food and pleasing to the eye, and also desirable for gaining wisdom, she took some and ate it. She also gave some to her husband, who was with her, and he ate it. ⁷ Then the eyes of both of them were opened, and they realized they were naked; so they sewed fig leaves together and made coverings for themselves.

⁸ Then the man and his wife heard the sound of the LORD God as he was walking in the garden in the cool of the day, and they hid from the LORD God among the trees of the garden.

7. *What did Satan promise would happen if Eve ate the forbidden fruit? What actually happened when she and Adam ate it? Explain.*

They would become god-like

Fear of the Lord.

8. *How would thankfulness have changed Eve's thought process when she "saw that the fruit of the tree was good for food and pleasing to the eye" (Genesis 3:6)?*

Be grateful for what was provided

without craving what was forbidden

9. *What are the things in your life—the things you want but don't have, or that you don't want but do have—that threaten to deprive you of thankfulness? What would a "thankful thought process" look like in your current situation?*

I'm grateful for all I've been given

10. *Take two minutes of silence to reread the passage, looking for a sentence, phrase, or even one word that stands out as something Jesus may want you to focus on in your life. If you're meeting with a group, the leader will keep track of time. At the end of two minutes, you may share your word or phrase with the group if you wish.*

11. *Read the passage aloud again. Take another two minutes of silence, prayerfully considering what response God might want you to make to what you have read in His Word. If you're meeting with a group, the leader will again keep track of time. At the end of two minutes, you may share what came to you in the silence if you wish.*

12. *What was it like for you to sit in silence with the passage? Did soaking it in like this help you understand it better than before?*

13. *If you're meeting with a group, how can the members pray for you? If you're using this study on your own, what would you like to say to God right now?*

_____

_____

_____

_____

LIVE IT

At the end of each session you'll find suggested Scripture readings for spending time alone with God during five days of the coming week. This week, the theme of each reading will focus on how you can be thankful for God's abundance in your life. Read each passage slowly, pausing to think about what is being said. Rather than approaching this as an assignment to complete, think of it as an opportunity to meet with the One who loves you most. Use any of the questions that are helpful.

Day 1

Read Ephesians 5:15–20. In this passage, Paul discusses the need to live wisely in the midst of evil days. What examples of wise living does he list?

_____

_____

_____

_____

Why is giving thanks for everything an example of wise living?

_____

_____

_____

_____

How is giving thanks the opposite of living foolishly?

_____

_____

_____

What's the importance of "always" giving thanks to God the Father "for everything" (verse 20)?

_____

_____

_____

_____

Each day this week, use a journal or separate sheet of paper to write down three things for which you are thankful. Doing this will help you focus more on what you *do* have rather than what you *do not* have, and it will make an impression on your heart. Ask God to help you grow wiser in the way you live by developing this consistent habit of thankfulness.

Day 2

Read Luke 9:16 and 22:17–19. Jesus had a habit of giving thanks over a meal before He distributed the food to others. Why do you think He did this?

Do you have a habit of giving thanks to God before you eat? Is this something you do whenever you eat . . . or only sometimes? Why?

How would it affect you if you gave thanks even over snacks, or when you brought groceries into your kitchen? Does that seem too extreme? Why or why not?

What are some other ways you could thank God, "whether in word or deed" (Colossians 3:17), more often as you go through your day?

Take a moment to thank God for the food you have eaten today and for the resources He has given to you. Remember in prayer those who are in need in your world.

Day 3

Read 2 Corinthians 9:6–11. In this passage, Paul discusses how your own generosity with what you have received from God can spark thankfulness in other people. Do you tend to think that you have received abundantly from Him and can afford to be generous with others? Or do you more often think that you have barely received enough and can't afford to be generous? Explain your thoughts.

What leads you to see your situation in either of these ways?

How does an attitude of abundance or scarcity affect your giving?

_____

_____

_____

Would you be likely to give more if you had a habit of greater thankfulness? Why or why not?

_____

_____

_____

Talk with God about your sense of abundance or scarcity and ask Him to help you see His provision from His perspective.

Day 4

Read 1 Timothy 4:1–5. In this passage, Paul warns against the idea (among other things) that Christians should abstain from certain foods because they are religiously impure. What does Paul have to say about such teachings (see verse 2)?

_____

_____

_____

In refuting this belief, what positive things does Paul say about the abundance God has made available?

Why does Paul emphasize thanksgiving twice (verses 3–4)?

What do you think Paul means when he says food is "consecrated by the word of God and prayer" (verse 5)? Why should that make us thankful?

Today, reflect on the idea that "everything God created is good, and nothing is to be rejected if it is received with thanksgiving" (verse 4). Thank God for the abundance of good things that He has created and put into your life.

Day 5

Read Daniel 6:6–10. During Daniel's time, a law was passed in Persia that no one could worship any god except the king for thirty days. However, even though Daniel was a high-ranking official in the king's court, he chose to ignore the law. Why do you think giving thanks to God multiple times a day was so important to him?

What are some possible reasons that Daniel opened his windows "toward Jerusalem" when he did this (verse 10)? Why didn't he try to conceal his actions if he knew they were against the law?

Why do you think Daniel couldn't just put off thanking God for thirty days?

How important is it for you to express thankfulness to God each day? Would you put it off for thirty days if the law required it? Why or why not?

Be intentional about setting aside at least three times during this day to thank God.

GIVING THANKS FOR GOD'S PROVISION

CONSIDER IT

The great enemy of thankfulness is *grumbling*, or feeling sorry for ourselves. Sometimes this takes the form of overt anger, while at other times it appears more like sadness. Grumbling is not godly sorrow but self-pity that resents what God has allowed to happen in our lives. In this session, we're going to take aim at self-pity and ask God to uproot it from our hearts.

1. *What does feeling sorry for yourself look like in your life?*

_____

_____

_____

2. *In what situations are you most likely to succumb to grumbling and self-pity?*

_____

_____

_____

EXPERIENCE IT

"Be on guard against the pit of self-pity. When you are weary or unwell, this demonic trap is the greatest danger you face. Don't even go near the edge of the pit. Its edges crumble easily, and before you know it, you are on the way down. It is ever so much harder to get out of the pit than to keep a safe distance from it. That is why I tell you to be on guard.

"There are several ways to protect yourself from self-pity. When you are occupied with praising and thanking Me, it is impossible to feel sorry for yourself. Also, the closer you live to Me, the more distance there is between you and the pit. Live in the Light of My Presence by *fixing your eyes on Me*. Then you will be able *to run with endurance the race that is set before you*, without stumbling or falling."

—From *Jesus Calling*, February 23

3. *What makes self-pity such a dangerous trap for believers in Christ?*

4. *How does thankfulness to God protect you from self-pity?*

"Let thankfulness temper all your thoughts. A thankful mind-set keeps you in touch with Me. I hate it when My children grumble, casually despising My sovereignty. Thankfulness is a safeguard against this deadly sin. Furthermore, a grateful attitude becomes a grid through which you perceive life. Gratitude enables you to see the Light of My Presence shining on all your circumstances. Cultivate a thankful heart, for this glorifies Me and fills you with Joy."

—From *Jesus Calling*, March 25

5. *What are some ways you can allow thankfulness to temper your thoughts? How can such a mind-set keep you in touch with God throughout the day?*

6. *In what ways can a grateful attitude become a grid through which you perceive life? Give an example of how this might work in practice.*

STUDY IT

Read aloud the following passage from Exodus 16:1–20, 31. The Israelites had formerly been slaves in Egypt, doing hard labor and making bricks to build a city. When the people cried out to God, He sent plagues against Egypt until Pharaoh allowed them to leave. The Lord then appointed Moses, along with his brother, Aaron, to lead the people out of Egypt. As the story picks up in this passage, the Israelites are crossing a desert region on the way to the fertile land that God promised to give them.

> [1] The whole Israelite community set out from Elim and came to the Desert of Sin, which is between Elim and Sinai, on the fifteenth day of the second month after they had come out of Egypt. [2] In the desert the whole community grumbled against Moses and Aaron. [3] The Israelites

said to them, "If only we had died by the Lord's hand in Egypt! There we sat around pots of meat and ate all the food we wanted, but you have brought us out into this desert to starve this entire assembly to death."

⁴ Then the Lord said to Moses, "I will rain down bread from heaven for you. The people are to go out each day and gather enough for that day. In this way I will test them and see whether they will follow my instructions. ⁵ On the sixth day they are to prepare what they bring in, and that is to be twice as much as they gather on the other days."

⁶ So Moses and Aaron said to all the Israelites, "In the evening you will know that it was the Lord who brought you out of Egypt, ⁷ and in the morning you will see the glory of the Lord, because he has heard your grumbling against him. Who are we, that you should grumble against us?" ⁸ Moses also said, "You will know that it was the Lord when he gives you meat to eat in the evening and all the bread you want in the morning, because he has heard your grumbling against him. Who are we? You are not grumbling against us, but against the Lord."

⁹ Then Moses told Aaron, "Say to the entire Israelite community, 'Come before the Lord, for he has heard your grumbling.'"

¹⁰ While Aaron was speaking to the whole Israelite community, they looked toward the desert, and there was the glory of the Lord appearing in the cloud.

¹¹ The Lord said to Moses, ¹² "I have heard the grumbling of the Israelites. Tell them, 'At twilight you will eat meat, and in the morning you will be filled with bread. Then you will know that I am the Lord your God.'"

¹³ That evening quail came and covered the camp, and in the morning there was a layer of dew around the camp. ¹⁴ When the dew was gone, thin flakes like frost on the ground appeared on the desert floor. ¹⁵ When the Israelites saw it, they said to each other, "What is it?" For they did not know what it was.

Moses said to them, "It is the bread the Lord has given you to eat. ¹⁶ This is what the Lord has commanded: 'Everyone is to gather as much as they need. Take an omer for each person you have in your tent.'"

¹⁷ The Israelites did as they were told; some gathered much, some little. ¹⁸ And when they measured it by the omer, the one who gathered much did not have too much, and the one who gathered little did not have too little. Everyone had gathered just as much as they needed.

¹⁹ Then Moses said to them, "No one is to keep any of it until morning."

²⁰ However, some of them paid no attention to Moses; they kept part of it until morning, but it was full of maggots and began to smell. So Moses was angry with them. . . .

³¹ The people of Israel called the bread manna. It was white like coriander seed and tasted like wafers made with honey.

7. *Under the Egyptians, the Israelites had been slaves who were beaten if they didn't meet their daily quota of bricks (see Exodus 5:6–18). Once they were freed, however, they remembered Egypt in a different light. What did they now say about their time there (see Exodus 16:3)? What attitude toward the past and the present do their words reflect?*

8. *Have you ever complained about the present in comparison with the past? If so, what did you complain about? If you're not typically a complainer, what are you sometimes tempted to complain about?*

9. *How did the Lord provide for His people in the desert? How has He provided for you?*

10. *Do you think it would be easier to be thankful for the Lord's provision if it fell miraculously from the sky every morning and you only had to gather it each day? Why or why not?*

11. *Take two minutes of silence to reread Exodus 16:2–4, looking for a sentence, phrase, or even one word that stands out as something Jesus may want you to focus on your life. If you're meeting with a group, the leader will keep track of time. At the end of two minutes, share your word or phrase with the group if you wish.*

12. *Read the passage aloud again. Take another two minutes of silence, prayerfully considering what response God might want you to make to what you have read in His Word. If you're meeting with a group, the leader will again keep track of time. At the end of two minutes, you may share what came to you in the silence if you wish.*

13. *If you're meeting with a group, how can the members pray for you? If you're using this study on your own, what would you like to say to God right now?*

LIVE IT

The theme of this week's daily Scripture readings is how to overcome grumbling and complaining. Read each passage slowly, pausing to think about what is being said. Rather than approaching this as an assignment to complete, think of it as an opportunity to meet with the One who loves you most. Use any of the questions that are helpful.

Day 1

Read Exodus 17:1–7. This story occurs right after the chapter in Exodus you studied this week, where God sent the miraculous manna to eat. Are you surprised the people so quickly returned to grumbling? Why or why not?

_____

_____

_____

_____

How understandable was their grumbling in this situation?

_____

_____

_____

_____

Why do you suppose God waited until the people were desperate before He provided water? What can we learn about God from this story?

_____

_____

_____

Has God ever waited until you were desperate before He provided for you?
Explain.

_____

_____

_____

_____

Each day this week, continue to write in a journal or on a separate sheet of paper three things for which you are thankful. Express to God today how grateful you are for the way He provides for your needs.

Day 2

Read Numbers 13:26–14:9. In this passage, you read how Moses sent twelve men into the Promised Land to survey it. The twelve returned with a unanimous report that the region was as fertile as God had promised—and ten of the twelve said the inhabitants of the land were too strong for the Israelites to overcome. Only Caleb and Joshua insisted that God would empower His people and give them victory. How did the Israelites respond to the surveyors' report?

_____

_____

_____

_____

Why weren't the people thankful that God was giving them a land that flowed with milk and honey?

What were Joshua and Caleb to see about the situation that the rest of the people were not? How did their attitude about God shape their opinions?

What are you tempted to grumble about today? How can you turn around and focus on what you are thankful for?

Tell God that you completely trust Him to lead you into a good place.

Day 3

Read Numbers 14:26–35. In this passage, you read how God responded to the people's grumbling when they complained about how hard it would be to conquer the Promised Land. What did God decide to do? What do you learn about Him from this response?

God made an exception for Caleb and Joshua because they had spoken up in favor of going in to conquer the land. What does it tell you about God that He made this exception?

Have you ever faced negative consequences of self-pity? If so, what happened?

Today, think about what God has given you to do and how you can respond to this task with trust and gratitude rather than fear and grumbling.

Day 4

Read Numbers 17:1–13. This story reveals what happened when the Israelites grumbled about the priesthood of Moses's brother, Aaron. What did God do to show that He had chosen Aaron to be the high priest?

How was grumbling against Aaron's leadership really grumbling against God?

How did the Israelites respond to the miracle of God (see verses 12–13)? Why do you suppose they weren't excited and drawn toward God?

What does this show about the people's perceptions of God? How might this scene have been different if the people had a humble, thankful attitude?

As you think about this story, consider your own temptations to grumble. Has this story helped you in any way when it comes to your tendency to complain? If so, how?

Day 5

Read Matthew 20:1–16. Jesus told this parable to show how God rewards those who serve Him, whether they begin serving Him as young people and are faithful all their lives, or they come to faith late in life and serve Him for a short time. What does it reveal about those who work in the vineyard from the first hour (see verse 11)? Why do they grumble?

Why does the owner of the vineyard reward each worker with the same payment?

Do you think the owner is unfair in doing this? Why or why not?

_____

_____

_____

Think of the most notorious sinner you know. How would you feel if that person came to faith late in life and was given the same welcome into God's kingdom as you are anticipating?

_____

_____

_____

If you have accepted Jesus as your Lord and Savior, consider what you can learn from this story about your thankfulness to God for *salvation*. Offer a prayer of gratitude to Him.

GIVING THANKS
FOR RESCUE

CONSIDER IT

There are many things we can thank God for in addition to His provision for our needs. Many of us have experienced times when God rescued us from a difficult situation and brought us to a place of safety and security. Remembering these experiences builds our trust in Him and reminds us of His goodness whenever life feels ordinary or frustrating. Recalling God's deliverance in past seasons of hardship can encourage us that He will be faithful when we face future adversity. In this session, we'll have a chance to reflect on some of these past experiences of rescue in our lives.

1. *On a scale of 1 to 5, how would you rate the level of well-being you are currently experiencing?*

1	2	③	4	5
Life is agonizingly hard right now				Life is absolutely fabulous right now

2. *How does the rating you gave yourself affect your inclination to be thankful?*

Not at all — always thankful
for God's blessings

EXPERIENCE IT

"*This is the day that I have made!* As you rejoice in this day of life, it will yield up to you precious gifts and beneficial training. Walk with Me along the high road of thanksgiving, and you will find all the delights I have made ready for you.

"To protect your thankfulness, you must remember that you reside in a fallen world, where blessings and sorrows intermingle freely. A constant focus on adversity defeats many Christians. They walk through a day that is brimming with beauty and brightness, seeing only the grayness of their thoughts. Neglecting the practice of giving thanks has darkened their minds. How precious are My children who remember to thank Me at all times. They can walk through the darkest days with Joy in their hearts because they know that the Light of My Presence is still shining on them. *Rejoice in this day that I have made*, for I am your steadfast Companion."

—FROM *JESUS CALLING*, NOVEMBER 26

3. *When you consider that today is the day the Lord has made for you, are you moved more toward joy and gratitude, toward resentment or disappointment, or toward a combination of those reactions?*

Joy and gratitude

4. *Does God's Presence with you in this day make it easier for you to be thankful? Or are you not so aware of His Presence as you go through your daily activities? How does your level of focus on adversity affect your awareness of God's Presence?*

I don't focus on the negative

"Let thankfulness rule in your heart. As you thank Me for blessings in your life, a marvelous thing happens. It is as if *scales fall off your eyes*, enabling you to see more and more of My glorious riches. With your eyes thus opened, you can help yourself to whatever you need from My treasure house. Each time you receive one of My golden gifts, let your thankfulness sing out praises to My Name. 'Hallelujahs' are the language of heaven, and they can become the language of your heart.

"A life of praise and thankfulness becomes a life filled with miracles. Instead of trying to be in control, you focus on Me and what I am doing. This is the power of praise: centering your entire being in Me. This is how I created you to live, for I made you in My own image. Enjoy abundant life by overflowing with praise and thankfulness."

—FROM *JESUS CALLING*, NOVEMBER 27

5. *Consider a time in your life when you experienced what felt like "scales" falling off your eyes" (see Acts 9:18) so you could see God's glorious riches. How did gratitude play a part?*

_____

_____

_____

6. *In what ways might "a life of praise and thankfulness [become] a life filled with miracles"?*

Awareness of God's blessings

_____

_____

STUDY IT

Read aloud the following passage from Psalm 107:1–32. In this song, an unknown poet expresses his gratitude to God for rescuing him from a series of misfortunes.

¹ Give thanks to the LORD, for he is good;
    his love endures forever.
² Let the redeemed of the LORD tell their story—
    those he redeemed from the hand of the foe,
³ those he gathered from the lands,
    from east and west, from north and south.
⁴ Some wandered in desert wastelands,
    finding no way to a city where they could settle.
⁵ They were hungry and thirsty,
    and their lives ebbed away.
⁶ Then they cried out to the LORD in their trouble,
    and he delivered them from their distress.
⁷ He led them by a straight way
    to a city where they could settle.
⁸ Let them give thanks to the LORD for his unfailing love
    and his wonderful deeds for mankind,
⁹ for he satisfies the thirsty
    and fills the hungry with good things.
¹⁰ Some sat in darkness, in utter darkness,
    prisoners suffering in iron chains,
¹¹ because they rebelled against God's commands
    and despised the plans of the Most High.
¹² So he subjected them to bitter labor;
    they stumbled, and there was no one to help.
¹³ Then they cried to the LORD in their trouble,
    and he saved them from their distress.

[14] He brought them out of darkness, the utter darkness,
and broke away their chains.

[15] Let them give thanks to the LORD for his unfailing love
and his wonderful deeds for mankind,

[16] for he breaks down gates of bronze
and cuts through bars of iron.

[17] Some became fools through their rebellious ways
and suffered affliction because of their iniquities.

[18] They loathed all food
and drew near the gates of death.

[19] Then they cried to the LORD in their trouble,
and he saved them from their distress.

[20] He sent out his word and healed them;
he rescued them from the grave.

[21] Let them give thanks to the LORD for his unfailing love
and his wonderful deeds for mankind.

[22] Let them sacrifice thank offerings
and tell of his works with songs of joy.

[23] Some went out on the sea in ships;
they were merchants on the mighty waters.

[24] They saw the works of the LORD,
his wonderful deeds in the deep.

[25] For he spoke and stirred up a tempest
that lifted high the waves.

[26] They mounted up to the heavens and went down to the depths;
in their peril their courage melted away.

[27] They reeled and staggered like drunkards;
they were at their wits' end.

[28] Then they cried out to the LORD in their trouble,
and he brought them out of their distress.

[29] He stilled the storm to a whisper;
the waves of the sea were hushed.

> ³⁰ They were glad when it grew calm,
>   and he guided them to their desired haven.
> ³¹ Let them give thanks to the LORD for his unfailing love
>   and his wonderful deeds for mankind.
> ³² Let them exalt him in the assembly of the people
>   and praise him in the council of the elders.

7. *In verses 2–3, the writer summarizes what all of the people mentioned in the psalm have in common: they have been rescued from some form of affliction and have been gathered into a better place. How is this true for each of the people in the verses below?*

verses 4–9	
verses 10–16	
verses 17–22	
verses 23–32	

8. *A repeated element in this psalm is, "Then they cried to the LORD in their trouble, and he saved them from their distress." When have you cried to the Lord in your trouble? How did He save you from your distress?*

9. *Another repeated element in this psalm is, "Let them give thanks to the* Lord *for his unfailing love and his wonderful deeds for mankind." Why is it so important to thank to the Lord when He rescues you from hardship? What's the purpose of remembering these experiences and reliving your gratitude?*

10. *The psalmist says, "Let the redeemed of the* Lord *tell their story" (verse 2). Below, briefly summarize a story of redemption from your life that you can share with the group. Why is it important to tell our stories?*

11. *Take two minutes of silence to reread Psalm 107:4–9, looking for a sentence, phrase, or even one word that stands out as something Jesus may want you to focus on in your life. If you're meeting with a group, the leader will keep track of time. At the end of two minutes, you may share your word or phrase with the group if you wish.*

V6 - They cried out to the Lord
and he brought them from their
distress

12. *Read the verses aloud again. Take another two minutes of silence, prayerfully considering what response God might want you to make to what you have read in His Word. If you're meeting with a group, the leader will again keep track of time. At the end of two minutes, you may share what came to you in the silence if you wish.*

_____

_____

_____

_____

13. *If you're meeting with a group, how can the members pray for you? If you're using this study on your own, what would you like to say to God right now?*

_____

_____

_____

_____

LIVE IT

The theme of this week's daily Scripture readings is expressing thankfulness to God for rescuing you from difficult situations. Read each passage slowly, pausing to think about what is being said. Rather than approaching this as an assignment to complete, think of it as an opportunity to meet with the One who loves you most. Use any of the questions that are helpful.

Day 1

Read Deuteronomy 26:1–11. What was the rite that God wanted the Israelites to perform each year at the beginning of the harvest season? What do you think the people were meant to learn from giving God the first portion of their harvest (firstfruits)?

What do you think the Israelites were meant to learn from telling the story God commanded them to tell in verses 5–10?

How is your story like this story? How is it different?

What would be the equivalent for you of offering a portion of your harvest to the Lord each year? What would this specifically look like in your life?

Tithing

Thank God today for leading you into a "good land." Make a plan to rejoice with others over the blessings you have received.

Day 2

Read Psalm 116:1–7. What is this psalmist's story? In what ways do you identify with him?

Perhaps right now you are only partway through this story in your life and the "cords of death" are still entangling you. If so, how do the psalmist's words affect you? Does this passage increase your hope? Does it make you wonder why you're not reaching safety more quickly? Explain.

What does the psalmist say to his soul in verse 7? How would you put this into your own words?

_____

_____

_____

_____

Why does the psalmist say his soul should be at rest? Is your soul at rest? Why or why not?

_____

_____

_____

Take some time to offer a prayer of thanks to God based on this psalm. Explain why you love the Lord and how He has answered your cry for mercy.

Day 3

Read Psalm 116:8–19. For what is the psalmist thankful? How does he express his gratitude?

_____

_____

_____

What would be a modern equivalent of lifting up the "cup of salvation" (verse 13)?

What would be a modern equivalent of sacrificing a "thank offering" (verse 17)?

What does it mean to "call on the name of the LORD" (verse 17)?

Between now and tomorrow, make a "thank offering" to God by recalling His past acts of mercy in your life and the way that He delivered you in your times of need.

Day 4

Read Psalm 118:1–7. Why do you think the psalmist repeats the phrase "his love endures forever" four times? Why is this such an important truth to rehearse and reflect on?

_____

_____

_____

For what is this psalmist thankful? How does he express his gratitude?

_____

_____

_____

For what are you thankful today? How are you expressing your gratitude?

_____

_____

_____

Can you say "his love endures forever" with conviction today? Why or why not?

_____

_____

_____

Today, ask God to open your eyes so you can witness signs of His enduring love for you.

Day 5

Read Psalm 118:15–21. For what is the psalmist thankful in these verses?

_____

_____

_____

_____

How would you describe his emotions? What key words or phrases stand out to you?

_____

_____

_____

How do the psalmist's words compare with your attitude toward God right now?

_____

_____

_____

How has God been active in your life during the past week? Where do you see Him at work?

_____

_____

_____

Say a prayer of thanksgiving to the Lord today—for He is good!

GIVING THANKS FOR TRIALS

CONSIDER IT

It's not too hard to acquire a habit of thanking God for the good things that happen in our lives. But thanking God for our trials, our problems, and the things that distress us comes only with discipline. Yet this is a good discipline to develop—no matter how difficult it may be—for the Bible tells us to count our trials as joyful and to give thanks in all things. In this session, we'll explore the reasons why God gives us this seemingly counterintuitive instruction, and we'll strive to begin to build the habit for ourselves.

1. *What is one trial you are currently facing? (It could be a physical ailment, a problem at work, a challenge in your family—anything that isn't going the way you wish it would.)*

2. *How have you seen God working in the midst of that trial? What have you been learning from the experience that you can be grateful for?*

EXPERIENCE IT

"Make friends with the problems in your life. Though many things feel random and wrong, remember that I am sovereign over everything. *I can fit everything into a pattern for good*, but only to the extent that you trust Me. Every problem can teach you something, transforming you little by little into the masterpiece I created you to be. The very same problem can become a stumbling block over which you fall, if you react with distrust and defiance. The choice is up to you, and you will have to choose many times each day whether to trust Me or defy Me.

"The best way to befriend your problems is to thank Me for them. This simple act opens your mind to the possibility of benefits flowing from your difficulties. You can even give persistent problems nicknames, helping you to approach them with familiarity rather than with dread. The next step is to introduce them to Me, enabling Me to embrace them in My loving Presence. I will not necessarily remove your problems, but My wisdom is sufficient to bring good out of every one of them."

—FROM *JESUS CALLING*, MARCH 5

3. *What are some reasons you should "make friends" with your problems?*

_____

_____

_____

_____

_____

4. *Would you say you typically react to problems with trust, defiance, or some other attitude? Think about how you are responding to a current problem in your life. Why are you leaning toward that particular reaction?*

"Thank Me for your problems. As soon as your mind gets snagged on a difficulty, bring it to Me with thanksgiving. Then ask Me to show you My way to handle the situation. The very act of thanking Me releases your mind from its negative focus. As you turn your attention to Me, the problem fades in significance and loses its power to trip you up. Together we can deal with the situation, either facing it head-on or putting it aside for later consideration.

"Most of the situations that entangle your mind are not today's concerns; you have borrowed them from tomorrow. In this case, I lift the problem out of today and deposit it in the future, where it is veiled from your eyes. In its place I give you My Peace, which flows freely from My Presence."

—FROM *JESUS CALLING*, MAY 11

5. *What part can thanksgiving play in the process of dealing with a problem?*

6. *Think of some of the problems that have been on your mind lately. Would you say these are problems for today or for tomorrow? What should you do if any of them are "borrowed . . . from tomorrow"?*

Study It

Read aloud the following passages from James 1:2–4 and Philippians 4:4–7. Note that the word "perseverance" in James 1:4 refers to the ability to hold up under the stress of your difficult circumstances with a right spiritual posture. The term "gentleness" in Philippians 4:5 refers to the habit of withholding retaliation against those who insult or harm you.

[2] Consider it pure joy, my brothers and sisters, whenever you face trials of many kinds, [3] because you know that the testing of your faith produces perseverance. [4] Let perseverance finish its work so that you may be mature and complete, not lacking anything (James 1:2–4).

[4] Rejoice in the Lord always. I will say it again: Rejoice! [5] Let your gentleness be evident to all. The Lord is near. [6] Do not be anxious about anything, but in every situation, by prayer and petition, with thanksgiving, present your requests to God. [7] And the peace of God, which transcends all understanding, will guard your hearts and your minds in Christ Jesus (Philippians 4:4–7).

7. *According to James, why should the people of God in particular rejoice when we face trials? How easy or hard is that for you to do?*

8. *What does Paul tell us in Philippians 4:4–7 to do in response to trials?*

9. *Why is thanksgiving such an important part of this response? What would your response consist of if you left out the rejoicing and the thanksgiving?*

10. *What's the connection between thanksgiving and peace in the passage from Philippians?*

11. *Take two minutes of silence to reread Philippians 4:4–7, looking for a sentence, phrase, or even one word that stands out as something Jesus may want you to focus on in your life. If you're meeting with a group, the leader will keep track of time. At the end of two minutes, you may share your word or phrase with the group if you wish.*

12. *Read the passage aloud again. Take another two minutes of silence, prayerfully considering what response God might want you to make to what you have read in His Word. If you're meeting with a group, the leader will again keep track of time. At the end of two minutes, you may share what came to you in the silence if you wish.*

13. *If you're meeting with a group, how can the members pray for you? If you're using this study on your own, what would you like to say to God right now?*

LIVE IT

The goal of this week's daily Scripture readings is to inspire you to offer thanksgiving to God even in the midst of your trials. Read each passage slowly, pausing to think about what is being said. Rather than approaching this as an assignment to complete, think of it as an opportunity to meet with the One who loves you most. Use any of the questions that are helpful.

Day 1

Read Romans 5:3–5. How are Paul's words in this passage similar to what James said in James 1:2–4? What additional instructions does Paul give?

_____

_____

_____

_____

If you are a Christian, in what ways has God's love been poured out in your heart through the Holy Spirit? How do you know that He is at work in your life?

_____

_____

_____

_____

How does the fact that God pours out His love to you in the midst of suffering affect your level of hope? Why do you need this kind of hope when you go through trials?

_____

_____

_____

How strong is your perseverance? How strong is your hope?

_____

_____

_____

Today, bring your request to God to build perseverance, character, and hope in your heart.

Day 2

Read 1 Peter 4:12–13. According to this passage, why should Christ's followers not be surprised when trials come their way? Why do you think some people are surprised when trials come?

_____

_____

_____

How do you respond to Peter's statement that a believer's trials enable him or her to share in Christ's suffering? How would your perspective change if you viewed your trials this way?

Why does Peter say Christians can rejoice when they participate in the sufferings of Christ?

What is a trial that you need to thank God for right now? How easy is it for you to do this?

Pause now and ask God to help you rejoice in the midst of whatever you are facing so that you may keep your focus on Him and His glory.

Day 3

Read 2 Corinthians 6:4–10. How do trials fit into Paul's picture of the way a servant of God displays his or her faith before the watching world?

Why would the way you handle trials as a believer affect the way nonbelievers think about Christ and about Christians in general?

How is it possible to be "sorrowful, yet always rejoicing" (verse 10)?

What would it look like for you to have an attitude of rejoicing in the midst of trials?

_____

_____

_____

Pray that God will help you have Paul's attitude toward trials throughout this day.

Day 4

Read 2 Corinthians 4:16–18. What does it mean to "lose heart"?

_____

_____

_____

_____

According to this passage, why is it that a Christian need never lose heart?

_____

_____

_____

_____

Does it help you to think of your affliction as light and momentary? Why or why not?

_____

_____

_____

_____

What is the "unseen" that you fix your eyes on? How does thanksgiving help you do that?

_____

_____

_____

Don't hesitate to tell God if you are tempted to lose heart. Seek His help in fixing your eyes on what is unseen.

Day 5

Read 2 Corinthians 12:9–10. Why does Paul say he is able to boast of his weaknesses?

_____

_____

_____

Why do you suppose God's power is made perfect in weakness? Have you ever experienced God working through you when you were weak? If so, describe that experience.

What is God's grace? How would you describe His grace in your life as a believer?

What do you think Paul means when he says, "For when I am weak, then I am strong" (verse 10)?

Ask God to open your eyes today to His grace in the midst of your weakness and need.

GIVING THANKS
FOR SPIRITUAL
BLESSINGS

CONSIDER IT

God provides for our physical needs: the food we eat, the water we drink, the roof over our heads. He provides the air we breathe and the earth on which we walk. He provides us with family, friends, education, and work. But most important of all, He meets our *spiritual* needs. His Son, Jesus, paid a great cost to meet these deepest needs of our soul—and when we recognize with gratitude what He has done, it allows us to be patient about our as-yet unfulfilled desires for this world. In this session, we'll look at some of our spiritual needs with the goal of growing in our gratitude for them.

1. *How would you describe the spiritual blessings God has given to you?*

_____

_____

_____

_____

2. *If you have accepted Jesus as your Savior, when were you first aware of the depths of God's mercy toward you in rescuing you from your sin? How did your story of faith begin?*

_____

_____

_____

_____

EXPERIENCE IT

"Rest in My Presence, allowing Me to take charge of this day. Do not bolt into the day like a racehorse suddenly released. Instead, walk purposefully with Me, letting Me direct your course one step at a time. Thank Me for each blessing along the way; this brings Joy to both you and Me. A grateful heart protects you from negative thinking. Thankfulness enables you to see the abundance I shower upon you daily. Your prayers and petitions are winged into heaven's throne room when they are permeated with thanksgiving. *In everything give thanks, for this is My will for you.*"

—FROM *JESUS CALLING*, FEBRUARY 25

3. *How does thankfulness encourage the habit of letting God be in charge of the day?*

_____

_____

_____

4. *How does a grateful heart protect you from negative thinking?*

_____

_____

_____

"Thank Me frequently as you journey through today. This practice makes it possible to *pray without ceasing*, as the apostle Paul taught. If you are serious about learning to pray continually, the best approach is to thank Me in every situation. These thankful prayers provide a solid foundation on which you can build all your other prayers. Moreover, a grateful attitude makes it easier for you to communicate with Me.

"When your mind is occupied with thanking Me, you have no time for worrying or complaining. If you practice thankfulness consistently, negative thought patterns will gradually grow weaker and weaker. *Draw near to Me* with a grateful heart, and My Presence will *fill you with Joy and Peace.*"

—From *Jesus Calling*, November 25

5. *What are the benefits of thanking God in every situation?*

---

6. *Do you have any negative thought patterns that you would like to have weakened by a habit of thankful thoughts? If so, what are those patterns?*

STUDY IT

Read aloud the following passage from Ephesians 1:3–14. Note that "spiritual blessing" (verse 3) means blessings received through connection with the Spirit of God (see verses 13–14). "Redemption" (verse 7) means buying back someone or something—such as buying a person out of slavery. Furthermore, Paul uses the male noun in the phrase "adoption to sonship" (verse 5) to indicate that all who welcome Christ into their lives are welcomed into a family relationship with God, with the full rights that Roman law gave to adult sons who were heirs.

[3] Praise be to the God and Father of our Lord Jesus Christ, who has blessed us in the heavenly realms with every spiritual blessing in Christ. [4] For he chose us in him before the creation of the world to be holy and blameless in his sight. In love [5] he predestined us for adoption to sonship through Jesus Christ, in accordance with his pleasure and will—[6] to the praise of his glorious grace, which he has freely given us in the One he loves. [7] In him we have redemption through his blood, the forgiveness of sins, in accordance with the riches of God's grace [8] that he lavished on us. With all wisdom and understanding, [9] he made known to us the mystery of his will according to his good pleasure, which he purposed in Christ, [10] to be put into effect when the times reach their fulfillment—to bring unity to all things in heaven and on earth under Christ.

[11] In him we were also chosen, having been predestined according to the plan of him who works out everything in conformity with the purpose of his will, [12] in order that we, who were the first to put our hope in Christ, might be for the praise of his glory. [13] And you also were included in Christ when you heard the message of truth, the gospel of your salvation. When you believed, you were marked in him with a seal, the promised Holy Spirit, [14] who is a deposit guaranteeing our inheritance until the redemption of those who are God's possession—to the praise of his glory.

7. *Review some of the spiritual blessings from this passage that Paul says have been afforded to every believer:*

- Being chosen to become holy and blameless
- Being adopted into God's family with the full rights of a son and heir

- Being redeemed out of slavery with Christ's blood
- Receiving God's grace as He lavishly gives Himself to you
- Receiving forgiveness of sins
- Being given God's plan to unify all things
- Receiving the Holy Spirit inside of you who makes every other blessing possible

Which of these stand out to you? How easy is it for you to connect with thankfulness for the things God has done for you? Why is it often easy to overlook these blessings?

8. *Paul repeats the phrase "the praise of his glory" in this passage. God's "glory" is the revelation of who He truly is, and when that is revealed, praise naturally follows. What can you learn about God from this passage that will lead you to thanksgiving and praise?*

9. *"In Christ" is another important phrase in these verses. As believers, God has blessed us in Christ, chosen us in Christ, and adopted us through Christ. To be "in Christ" is to be connected to Him, drawing our very life from Him. Why should believers be thankful for being "in Christ"?*

10. *What would help you become more deeply thankful for being chosen and adopted into God's family, bought out of slavery, and brought into intimate connection with Christ?*

11. *Take two minutes of silence to reread the passage, looking for a sentence, phrase, or even one word that stands out as something Jesus may want you to focus on in your life. If you're meeting with a group, the leader will keep track of time. At the end of two minutes, you may share your word or phrase with the group if you wish.*

12. *Read the passage aloud again. Take another two minutes of silence, prayerfully considering what response God might want you to make to what you have read in His Word. If you're meeting with a group, the leader will again keep track of time. At the end of two minutes, you may share what came to you in the silence if you wish.*

13. *If you're meeting with a group, how can the members pray for you? If you're using this study on your own, what would you like to say to God right now?*

LIVE IT

The theme of this week's daily Scripture readings is expressing your thankfulness to God for the spiritual blessings He has supplied. Read each passage slowly, pausing to think about what is being said. Rather than approaching this as an assignment to complete, think of it as an opportunity to meet with the One who loves you most. Use any of the questions that are helpful.

Day 1

Read Colossians 1:12–14. For what does Paul urge the people of God to give thanks to the Father?

_____

_____

_____

_____

What is the "kingdom of light"? What do you know about it?

_____

_____

_____

_____

What is the "dominion of darkness"? Why should Christians be thankful to be rescued from it?

_____

_____

_____

_____

How thankful are you for this rescue? What helps you to be thankful? What gets in the way?

_____

_____

_____

Today, talk with God about the amazing thing He has done for you by including you in the kingdom of light.

Day 2

Read Ephesians 1:18–20. In this passage, Paul prays that the eyes of the believers' hearts may be enlightened. How would this promote your gratitude to God?

_____

_____

_____

What is the hope to which God has called you as a disciple of Christ? Why should you be thankful for that hope?

_____

_____

_____

_____

What is the "inheritance" God has waiting for His children? Why should we be thankful for it?

How does Paul describe the power at work on a believer's behalf? Why should that make God's people thankful?

Choose one item from this passage and pour out your thankfulness about it to God.

Day 3

Read Ephesians 2:1–10. How would you describe the condition of those who are spiritually dead? What does it mean to be "alive in Christ" (verse 5)?

What does it mean to say that believers are seated with Christ in the heavenly realms (see verse 6)? Chew on this for a while, and then explain why it makes you thankful.

_____

_____

_____

What is the connection between grace (verses 4, 8) and gratitude?

_____

_____

_____

How will you express your gratitude to God for His grace in your life?

_____

_____

_____

Thank God for rescuing you from the bondage to "the ruler of the kingdom of the air" (verse 2).

Day 4

Read Hebrews 12:28–29. What does it mean to say that God's kingdom "cannot be shaken"?

_____

_____

_____

_____

What else do you know about God's kingdom? Why should you be thankful for it?

_____

_____

_____

_____

Why does God deserve to be worshiped with reverence and awe?

_____

_____

_____

_____

What does it mean to say that He is "a consuming fire" (verse 29)? When you think of God as a consuming fire, does that inspire you to gratitude? Why or why not?

Approach God with awe today, expressing thanks that He has made it possible for every believer to safely and intimately approach Him.

Day 5

Read Colossians 4:2–6. What is watchfulness in prayer? Why is it important?

How does watchfulness in prayer go along with thankfulness in prayer?

The "mystery of Christ" (verse 3) is the revealed secret that Christ has come to dwell in the Gentiles and not just the Jews. Why is that something for which you can be thankful?

_____

_____

_____

How thankful are you for the wonder of what God has done in Christ? What would help you grow in your gratitude for that?

_____

_____

_____

Pour out your thanks to God in this moment for all the spiritual blessings He has provided.

GIVING THANKS
FOR THE CROSS

CONSIDER IT

When nothing seems to be going our way, we can easily stray into feelings of self-pity and ask questions such as, "Jesus, what have You done for me lately?" Chances are that He's done a lot for us *lately* that we aren't noticing. However, even more than that, He has done things for us *in the past* that should arouse our profound gratitude—even if He never did anything else. One of the greatest things He has done is go to the cross for us. In this session, we'll take a close look at Jesus on the cross to let that event soak into our hearts.

1. *How old were you when you first heard about Jesus dying on a cross for you?*

_____

_____

_____

2. *How did you respond to the message? Was it difficult for you to accept? Explain.*

_____

_____

_____

EXPERIENCE IT

"As you sit quietly in My Presence, let Me fill your heart and mind with thankfulness. This is the most direct way to achieve a thankful stance. If your mind needs a focal point, gaze at My Love poured out for you on the cross. Remember that *nothing in heaven or on earth can separate you from that Love*. This remembrance builds a foundation of gratitude in you, a foundation that circumstances cannot shake.

"As you go through this day, look for tiny treasures strategically placed along the way. I lovingly go before you and plant little pleasures to brighten your day. Look carefully for them, and pluck them one by one. When you reach the end of the day, you will have gathered a lovely bouquet. Offer it up to Me with a grateful heart. Receive My Peace as you lie down to sleep, with thankful thoughts playing a lullaby in your mind."

—FROM *JESUS CALLING*, NOVEMBER 23

3. *Why is it helpful to focus on Jesus' Love poured out on the cross when you are sitting quietly in His presence?*

4. *How solid is your belief as a child of God that nothing can separate you from Jesus' Love?*

"Thank Me for the very things that are troubling you. You are on the brink of rebellion, precariously close to shaking your fist in My Face. You are tempted to indulge in just a little complaining about My treatment of you. But once you step over that line, torrents of rage and self-pity can sweep you away. The best protection against this indulgence is thanksgiving. It is impossible to thank Me and curse Me at the same time.

"Thanking Me for trials will feel awkward and contrived at first. But if you persist, your thankful words, prayed in faith, will eventually make a difference in your heart. Thankfulness awakens you to My Presence, which overshadows all your problems."

—FROM *JESUS CALLING*, JUNE 22

5. *Have you ever been "precariously close to shaking your fist" in Jesus' Face? If so, what were the circumstances? What was the result?*

_____

_____

_____

6. *Why is it important to persist in thanking God in your trials?*

_____

_____

_____

STUDY IT

Read aloud the following passage from Matthew 27:32–50. This scene takes place just after Jesus was tried and sentenced by the Roman governor at the request of the Jewish leaders in Jerusalem. As you read, note that crucifixion was a barbaric method of execution. It was so grotesque that it was never used on Roman citizens, but was reserved for prisoners whom the Romans wanted to denigrate. The gall that Jesus refused (verse 34) was a mild painkiller given by the merciful to those being crucified.

Matthew doesn't describe all the details of crucifixion because his first readers would have been very familiar with this slow and painful form of death. However, we know that victims were nailed by the wrists and ankles to wooden crosspieces, which meant they had to push up with their feet every time they wanted to take a breath. Ultimately, death came from suffocation once a victim became too weak to lift himself.

[32] As they were going out, they met a man from Cyrene, named Simon, and they forced him to carry the cross. [33] They came to a place called Golgotha (which means "the place of the skull"). [34] There they offered Jesus wine to drink, mixed with gall; but after tasting it, he refused to drink it. [35] When they had crucified him, they divided up his clothes by casting lots. [36] And sitting down, they kept watch over him there. [37] Above his head they placed the written charge against him: THIS IS JESUS, THE KING OF THE JEWS.

[38] Two rebels were crucified with him, one on his right and one on his left. [39] Those who passed by hurled insults at him, shaking their heads [40] and saying, "You who are going to destroy the temple and build it in three days, save yourself! Come down from the cross, if you are the Son of God!" [41] In the same way the chief priests, the teachers of the law and the elders mocked him. [42] "He saved others," they said, "but he can't save himself! He's the king of Israel! Let him come down now from the cross, and we will believe in him. [43] He trusts in God. Let God rescue him now if he wants him, for he said, 'I am the Son of God.'" [44] In the same way the rebels who were crucified with him also heaped insults on him.

[45] From noon until three in the afternoon darkness came over all the land. [46] About three in the afternoon Jesus cried out in a loud voice, *"Eli, Eli, lema sabachthani?"* (which means "My God, my God, why have you forsaken me?").

⁴⁷ When some of those standing there heard this, they said, "He's calling Elijah."

⁴⁸ Immediately one of them ran and got a sponge. He filled it with wine vinegar, put it on a staff, and offered it to Jesus to drink. ⁴⁹ The rest said, "Now leave him alone. Let's see if Elijah comes to save him."

⁵⁰ And when Jesus had cried out again in a loud voice, he gave up his spirit.

7. *Why do you think Jesus refused to drink the gall (see verse 34)?*

_____

_____

_____

_____

8. *The bystanders said, "Come down from the cross, if you are the Son of God" (verse 40). Was Jesus able to do this? Why or why not? Why does this matter?*

_____

_____

_____

_____

9. *Jesus cried out, "My God, my God, why have you forsaken me?" (verse 46). This is the first line of Psalm 22, in which David goes on to express great trust in God as well as great agony. David also expresses what Jesus felt when He took our sin on Himself and felt distance from His Father for the first time. Think about what He was going through. How does that move you to respond?*

10. *Why should we be thankful for Jesus' suffering and death on the cross?*

11. *Take two minutes of silence to reread Matthew 27:39–46, looking for a sentence, phrase, or even one word that stands out as something Jesus may want you to focus on in your life. If you're meeting with a group, the leader will keep track of time. At the end of two minutes, you may share your word or phrase with the group if you wish.*

12. *Read the passage aloud again. Take another two minutes of silence, prayerfully considering what response God might want you to make to what you have read in His Word. If you're meeting with a group, the leader will again keep track of time. At the end of two minutes, you may share what came to you in the silence if you wish.*

13. *If you're meeting with a group, how can the members pray for you? If you're using this study on your own, what would you like to say to God right now?*

LIVE IT

The theme of this week's daily readings is expressing thankfulness to Jesus for what He did on the cross on every sinner's behalf. Read each passage slowly, pausing to think about what is being said. Rather than approaching this as an assignment to complete, think of it as an opportunity to meet with the One who loves you most. Use any of the questions that are helpful.

Day 1

Read Colossians 1:15–20. How does Paul describe Jesus' greatness in this passage? Which truth about Jesus strikes you as most significant today? Why?

_____

_____

_____

_____

How does Jesus' shed blood reconcile all things to God? Why were those things formerly separated from God?

_____

_____

_____

_____

If you are a Christian, can you relate to the idea of having been estranged from God, but now brought into a relationship of peace? In what way?

_____

_____

_____

_____

Do you tend to take peace with God for granted, or do you tend to be thankful for it? Explain.

Offer praise to Jesus for what this passage says about Him, thanking Him for what He did for you on the cross.

Day 2

Read Colossians 2:13–15. What did God do to rescue those who were dead in their sins? How have you experienced being alive in Christ?

Do you ever think about God nailing the list of your sin-caused debts to the cross and declaring them paid for? Picture that, and then describe how it makes you want to respond.

How do you react to the idea that Jesus has disarmed the demonic powers and authorities?

_____

_____

_____

What are you most thankful for in this passage?

_____

_____

_____

If you have accepted God's gift of salvation, offer your thanks and praise to Him for making you alive in Christ, forgiving your sins, and triumphing over the powers of darkness.

Day 3

Read Romans 3:23–26. Paul writes that God presented Christ as a "sacrifice of atonement" (verse 25 NIV) or "propitiation" (ESV)? In other words, God offered His Son in our place to pay the penalty for our sins. Why is this something to be deeply thankful for?

_____

_____

_____

What would have happened to you because of your sin if God hadn't presented Jesus as an atoning sacrifice for you?

To be "justified" means to be considered righteous in God's eyes (see verse 24)? Why should you be thankful for this work of Christ's?

How does understanding the meaning of these theological words draw you deeper into the wonder of what Jesus has done?

Go to God for a deeper understanding of what Jesus did for sinners on the cross, and let your thankfulness well up from inside you.

Day 4

Read 1 Peter 2:23–25. How does it affect you to think about the fact that Jesus didn't retaliate when He was insulted and tortured?

How does it affect you to know that he bore the worst of your sins on the cross?

How were you like a sheep going astray?

One way you show your thankfulness to Christ is by dying to sin and living for righteousness (see verse 24). What does it mean to die to sin? Can you say you have you been healed by Jesus' wounds? How has this been true for you?

Say a prayer of thanks to the Good Shepherd for drawing you close to Him through His sacrifice on the cross.

Day 5

Read Romans 5:6–8. In what way were you powerless before Christ died for you?

Why is it extraordinary that Jesus decided to die for you—an "unrighteous" person?

What does it reveal about God that He chose to send His Son to die for all sinners? If you have accepted this gift, how should it lead to thankfulness regardless of your circumstances?

_____

_____

_____

Take some time today to reflect on who you have been at your worst. Offer thanks and praise to Jesus for being willing to intervene on your behalf at that very time.

GIVING THANKS FOR THE RESURRECTION

CONSIDER IT

Jesus died to pay for our sins, and He rose from the dead as evidence that the price was paid in full. His resurrection declared that He had conquered death and that His followers, too, would one day rise to life again after their own deaths. Jesus' resurrection makes it possible for anyone to die to sin and live a new life in intimate connection with Jesus. In fact, His resurrection accomplished so much good that we celebrate it every Sunday. In this session, we'll reflect on the resurrection and seek to deepen our thankfulness for this most amazing event.

1. *Why is it important that Jesus not only died for humanity's sin but also rose from the grave?*

_____

_____

_____

2. *What are some ways (outside of Easter events) that you and your church celebrate the resurrection?*

_____

_____

_____

EXPERIENCE IT

"Draw near to Me with a thankful heart, aware that your cup is overflowing with blessings. Gratitude enables you to perceive Me more clearly and to rejoice in our Love-relationship. *Nothing can separate you from My loving Presence!* That is the basis of your security. Whenever you start to feel anxious, remind yourself that your security rests in Me alone, and I am totally trustworthy.

"You will never be in control of your life circumstances, but you can relax and trust in My control. Instead of striving for a predictable, safe lifestyle, seek to know Me in greater depth and breadth. I long to make your life a glorious adventure, but you must stop clinging to old ways. I am always doing something new within My beloved ones. Be on the lookout for all that I have prepared for you."

—FROM *JESUS CALLING*, JULY 5

3. *Why do you suppose gratitude helps you perceive Jesus more clearly?*

_____

_____

_____

4. *As a believer, how easy is it for you to relax and trust in Jesus' control of your situation? What helps you do that? What gets in the way?*

_____

_____

_____

"Come to Me for all that you need. Come into My Presence with thanksgiving, for thankfulness opens the door to My treasures. When you are thankful, you affirm the central truth that I am Good. I am Light, in *whom there is no darkness at all.* The assurance that I am entirely Good meets your basic need for security. Your life is not subject to the whims of a sin-stained deity.

"Relax in the knowledge that the One who controls your life is totally trustworthy. Come to Me with confident expectation. There is nothing you need that I cannot provide."

—From *Jesus Calling*, May 5

5. *Why is it so important to be convinced that God is good?*

_____

_____

_____

_____

6. *What evidence do you have that the One who controls your life is totally trustworthy? How is the resurrection evidence of Jesus' trustworthiness?*

_____

_____

_____

Study It

Read aloud the following passage from 1 Corinthians 15:14–24. In this passage, Paul explains some of what the resurrection means for those who believe in Christ. As you read, note that "firstfruits" (verses 20, 23) refers to the first portion of a harvest, while "dominion, authority and power" (verse 24) refers to the demonic powers.

[14] If Christ has not been raised, our preaching is useless and so is your faith. [15] More than that, we are then found to be false witnesses about God, for we have testified about God that he raised Christ from the dead. . . . [17] And if Christ has not been raised, your faith is futile; you are still in your sins. [18] Then those also who have fallen asleep in Christ are lost. [19] If only for this life we have hope in Christ, we are of all people most to be pitied.

[20] But Christ has indeed been raised from the dead, the firstfruits of those who have fallen asleep. [21] For since death came through a man, the resurrection of the dead comes also through a man. [22] For as in Adam all die, so in Christ all will be made alive. [23] But each in turn: Christ, the firstfruits; then, when he comes, those who belong to him. [24] Then the end will come, when he hands over the kingdom to God the Father after he has destroyed all dominion, authority and power.

7. *Why is the Christian faith futile without the resurrection (see verse 17)? Why is every follower of Christ still in his or her sins if the resurrection didn't happen?*

_____

_____

_____

8. *Because Christ was raised from the dead, believers can look forward to rising to life again after they die. They are destined for a new heaven and a new earth (see Revelation 21). How do you imagine your ultimate destiny? How attractive to you is that picture?*

_____

_____

_____

9. *Why does Paul say, "If only for this life we have hope in Christ, we are of all people most to be pitied" (verse 19)? Why are those who have this type of "hope" to be pitied?*

---

10. *What does it mean to say that Christ is "the firstfruits of those who have fallen asleep" (verse 20)? Why should believers be thankful for Jesus' resurrection and their own future resurrection?*

---

11. *Take two minutes of silence to reread 1 Corinthians 15:14–19, looking for a sentence, phrase, or even one word that stands out as something Jesus may want you to focus on in your life. If you're meeting with a group, the leader will keep track of time. At the end of two minutes, you may share your word or phrase with the group if you wish.*

---

12. *Read the passage aloud again. Take another two minutes of silence, prayerfully considering what response God might want you to make to what you have read in His Word. If you're meeting with a group, the leader will again keep track of time. At the end of two minutes, you may share with the group what came to you in the silence if you wish.*

_____

_____

_____

_____

13. *If you're meeting with a group, how can the members pray for you? If you're using this study on your own, what would you like to say to God right now?*

_____

_____

_____

_____

LIVE IT

The theme of this week's daily Scripture reading is on expressing gratitude to Jesus for the resurrection. Read each passage slowly, pausing to think about what is being said. Rather than approaching this as an assignment to complete, think of it as an opportunity to meet with the One who loves you most. Use any of the questions that are helpful.

Day 1

Read Luke 24:1–8. Imagine being one of these women going to the tomb. What do you see? What do you hear? What do you feel?

Why do you suppose the women didn't expect Jesus' resurrection, even though He had promised it?

Why weren't these women immediately thankful?

How does this story affect you now? How easy is it for you to get to a place of wonder and gratitude for this event? Explain.

Today, go to God with your honest response to Jesus' resurrection.

Day 2

Read Romans 6:4–11. If you are a believer in Christ, how have you already experienced death and resurrection with Him?

What has been your experience of new life in Jesus? In what ways is your death and resurrection yet to come?

In what sense has Jesus conquered death? What are the results of that conquest for your life?

How can you live in light of the fact that Jesus has defeated death? How can you count yourself dead to sin this week? What does it mean to be dead to sin?

Seek God's help in counting yourself "dead to sin."

Day 3

Read Luke 24:36–49. Imagine yourself as one of the people in this scene. What do you see? What do you hear? What do you feel? What do you do?

How did Jesus prove that He wasn't a ghost? What understanding about the nature of a resurrected body do you gain from this account?

What was the point of Jesus showing His followers His hands and feet (see verse 40)? Imagine seeing those hands and feet. How do you respond?

Talk with God today about your thankfulness that Jesus' resurrected hands and feet still show the scars of His crucifixion.

Day 4

Read Colossians 2:9–15. Why does Paul describe baptism as a burial (see verse 12)? How is baptism also a resurrection?

How does Paul describe what God has done for His children in verses 13–14? How does the resurrection put the demonic powers to shame?

What are you thankful for as you read this passage? List as many things as possible.

Why are you thankful for those things you listed? How do they make a difference to your life here and now?

Offer thanks and praise to God for what He has done for you through Jesus' death and resurrection.

Day 5

Read Matthew 28:1–10. How is Matthew's version of Jesus' resurrection similar to Luke's account in Luke 24:1–8? How is it different?

What additional information do we learn from Matthew's account?

The angel rolled the stone away from the mouth of the tomb not to let Jesus out (He was already gone) but to show the women that He had risen. Why was it important for them to see the empty tomb? Why was it necessary for the angel to tell the women not to be afraid?

Would you have been afraid if this happened to you? Why or why not?

_____

_____

_____

Express to God what you're thankful for today as you read this story.

GIVING THANKS FOR THE HOLY SPIRIT

CONSIDER IT

When many of us think about the Holy Spirit—if we think of Him at all—we picture Him as an impersonal force, like electricity. However, the Holy Spirit is a Person, just as Jesus is a Person. The Holy Spirit is the Presence of Jesus with every believer at every moment, teaching them and empowering them to do the things they were put on earth to do. In this final session, we'll explore who the Holy Spirit is and take time to be thankful for His strengthening Presence.

1. *What comes to your mind when you think of the Holy Spirit?*

_____

_____

_____

2. *How would you define the Holy Spirit's role in your life?*

_____

_____

_____

EXPERIENCE IT

"Thank Me for the glorious gift of My Spirit. This is like priming the pump of a well. As you bring Me the sacrifice of thanksgiving, regardless of your feelings, My Spirit is able to work more freely within you. This produces more thankfulness and more freedom, until you are overflowing with gratitude.

"I shower blessings on you daily, but sometimes you don't perceive them. When your mind is stuck on a negative focus, you see neither Me nor My gifts. In faith, thank Me for whatever is preoccupying your mind. This will clear the blockage so that you can find Me."

—FROM *JESUS CALLING*, MARCH 20

3. *Why do you think the Holy Spirit is freer to work within God's children when they are thankful to Him?*

_____

_____

_____

4. *"When your mind is stuck on a negative focus, you see neither Me nor My gifts." To what degree can you relate to this statement? Do you ever get stuck on a negative focus? What can you do when it happens?*

_____

_____

_____

"I am calling you to a life of thankfulness. I want all your moments to be punctuated with thanksgiving. The basis for your gratitude is My sovereignty. I am the Creator and Controller of the universe. Heaven and earth are filled with My glorious Presence.

"When you criticize or complain, you are acting as if you think *you* could run the world better than I do. From your limited human perspective, it may look as if I'm mismanaging things. But you don't know what I know or see what I see. If I pulled back the curtain to allow you to view heavenly realms, you would understand much more. However, I have designed you to *live by faith, not by sight.* I lovingly shield you from knowing the future or seeing into the spirit world. Acknowledge My sovereignty by *giving thanks in all circumstances."*

—FROM *JESUS CALLING*, APRIL 16

5. *What is God's sovereignty? How is it the basis for your gratitude?*

6. *Why is complaining a denial of God's sovereignty? Think of an instance when you criticized or complained. Were you forgetting God's sovereignty or purposely complaining about His sovereignty?*

STUDY IT

Read aloud the following passage from John 14:15–18, 25–27. Note that the word *advocate* in verses 16 and 26 means "one who comes alongside to help," like a legal advocate in court.

¹⁵ "If you love me, keep my commands. ¹⁶ And I will ask the Father, and he will give you another advocate to help you and be with you forever— ¹⁷ the Spirit of truth. The world cannot accept him, because it neither sees

him nor knows him. But you know him, for he lives with you and will be in you. ¹⁸ I will not leave you as orphans; I will come to you. . . .

²⁵ "All this I have spoken while still with you. ²⁶ But the Advocate, the Holy Spirit, whom the Father will send in my name, will teach you all things and will remind you of everything I have said to you. ²⁷ Peace I leave with you; my peace I give you. I do not give to you as the world gives. Do not let your hearts be troubled and do not be afraid."

7. *What connection does Jesus draw in verses 15–16 between loving Him, obeying Him, and receiving the Holy Spirit?*

8. *What do you learn about the Holy Spirit by thinking of Him as your Advocate?*

9. *What are your expectations of how the Holy Spirit can work through you as a believer in Christ? In what ways do you tend to limit the Holy Spirit by your expectations?*

10. *As a follower of Christ, you can grow closer to the Holy Spirit simply by asking the Father to fill you with His Spirit (see Acts 4:31; Ephesians 5:18). How do you respond to the idea of asking God daily (or even hourly) to fill you with His Spirit? Why does that idea attract you or not?*

11. *Take two minutes of silence to reread the passage, looking for a sentence, phrase, or even one word that stands out as something Jesus may want you to focus on in your life. If you're meeting with a group, the leader will keep track of time. At the end of two minutes, you may share your word or phrase with the group if you wish.*

12. *Read the passage aloud again. Take another two minutes of silence, prayerfully considering what response God might want you to make to what you have read in His Word. If you're meeting with a group, the leader will again keep track of time. At the end of two minutes, you may share what came to you in the silence if you wish.*

13. *If you're meeting with a group, how can the members pray for you? If you're using this study on your own, what would you like to say to God right now?*

LIVE IT

The goal of this week's daily Scripture readings is to inspire you to live the Christian life with boldness in the power of the Holy Spirit. Read each passage slowly, pausing to think about what is being said. Rather than approaching this as an assignment to complete, think of it as an opportunity to meet with the One who loves you most. Use any of the questions that are helpful.

Day 1

Read John 16:12–15. What does Jesus say here about what the Holy Spirit does for believers?

What do you learn from this passage about the relations between the Father, Jesus, and the Holy Spirit?

_____

_____

_____

_____

Why is it so important for us to know the truth?

_____

_____

_____

_____

What sort of truth do you think Jesus is talking about here? What truth has the Spirit made known to you since you accepted Christ?

_____

_____

_____

_____

Today, thank the Holy Spirit for guiding you into all truth.

Day 2

Read Romans 8:5–8. What does it mean to live in accordance with the Holy Spirit?

What does Paul say about the mind governed by the Spirit?

What are some of the things the Spirit desires? How can you set your mind on those things?

As a follower of Christ, what does this passage say that makes you grateful for the Holy Spirit's work in your life?

_____

_____

_____

_____

Take a few minutes to praise Jesus for sending His Spirit to you.

Day 3

Read Romans 8:9–11. What does Paul say about the importance of having the Holy Spirit living in you?

_____

_____

_____

_____

Living in the "realm of the flesh" (verse 9) means living a life controlled by one's lower impulses. What does this look like in practical terms?

_____

_____

_____

Why should Christians be grateful that they no longer live in the realm of the flesh?

_____

_____

_____

_____

What is the connection between the Holy Spirit and a believer's hope of resurrection?

_____

_____

_____

Today, thank the Holy Spirit for allowing you to live in Him and for the hope of bodily resurrection you can have when He lives in you.

Day 4

Read Romans 8:12–17. How, in practical terms, do you put to death the misdeeds of the body? How does the Holy Spirit help believers do that?

_____

_____

_____

What is the difference between being slaves and being God's children? What does the Holy Spirit have to do with a believer's adoption as one of God's children?

_____

_____

What does the Spirit testify about believers (see verse 16)? Why are you thankful for that?

_____

_____

What does it mean to be a co-heir with Christ? If you belong to Jesus, what are you going to inherit?

_____

_____

_____

Express thanks to God for the Holy Spirit, who assures believers they really are God's children and a part of His family.

Day 5

Read Acts 13:1–12. What does the Holy Spirit do in verse 2? In verse 4? In verses 9–11?

Why do you suppose the Holy Spirit chose to speak while the leaders in Antioch were worshiping the Lord and fasting?

Do you believe the Holy Spirit works in these ways today? Why or why not?

What does this tell you about the Spirit?

_____

_____

_____

In Romans 10:9, Paul writes, "If you declare with your mouth, 'Jesus is Lord,' and believe in your heart that God raised him from the dead, you will be saved." As you conclude this study, thank God for giving you this incredible offer of salvation and for allowing you to be part of His work on this earth. Also thank God for the Holy Spirit's work in every generation and in your own life as a follower of Christ.

LEADER'S NOTES

Thank you for your willingness to lead a group through this *Jesus Calling* study. The rewards of leading are different from the rewards of participating, and we hope you find your own walk with Jesus deepened by this experience. In many ways, your group meetings will be structured like other Bible studies in which you've participated. You'll want to open in prayer, for example, and ask people to silence their phones. These leader's notes will focus on elements of the study that may be new to you.

CONSIDER IT

This first portion of the study functions as an icebreaker. It gets the group members thinking about the topic at hand by asking them to share from their own experience. Some people may be tempted to tell a long story in response to one of these questions, but the goal is to keep the answers brief. Ideally, you want everyone in the group to have a chance to answer the *Consider It* questions, so you may want to explain up front that everyone needs to limit his or her answer to one minute.

With the rest of the study, it is generally not a good idea to go around the circle and have everyone answer every question—a free-flowing discussion is more desirable. But with the *Consider It* questions, you can go around the circle. Encourage shy people to share, but don't force them. Tell the group they should feel free to pass if they prefer not to answer a question.

Experience It

This is the group's chance to talk about excerpts from the *Jesus Calling* devotional. You will need to monitor this discussion closely so that you have enough time for the actual study of God's Word that follows. If the group has a long and rich discussion on one of the devotional excerpts, you may choose to skip the other one and move on to the Bible study. Don't feel obliged to cover every *Experience It* question if the conversation is fruitful. On the other hand, do move on if the group gets off on a tangent.

Study It

Try to do the *Study It* exercise in session 1 on your own before the group meets the first time so you can coach people on what to expect. Note that this section may be a little different from Bible studies your group has done in the past. The group will talk about the Bible passage as usual, but then there will be several minutes of silence so individuals can pray about what God might want to say to them personally through the reading. It will be up to you to keep track of the time and call people back together when the time is up. (There are some good timer apps that play a gentle chime or other pleasant sound instead of a disruptive noise.) If the group members aren't used to being silent in a "crowd," brief them on what to expect.

Don't be afraid to let people sit in silence. Two minutes of quiet may seem like a long time at first, but it will help to train group members to sit in silence with God when they are alone. They can remain where they are in the circle, or if you have space, you can let them go off by themselves to other rooms at your instruction. If your group meets in a home, ask the host before the meeting which rooms are available for use. Some people will be more comfortable in the quiet if they have a bit of space from others.

When the group reconvenes after the time of silence, invite them to share what they experienced. There are several questions provided in this study guide that you can ask. Note that it's not necessary to cover every question if the group has a good discussion going. It's also not necessary to go around the circle and make everyone share.

Don't be concerned if the group members are reserved and slow to share after the exercise. People are often quiet when they are pulling together their ideas, and the exercise will have been a new experience for many of them. Just ask a question and let it hang in the air until someone speaks up. You can then say, "Thank you. What about others? What came to you when you sat with the passage?"

Some people may say they found it hard to quiet their minds enough to focus on the passage for those few minutes. Tell them this is okay. They're practicing a skill, and sometimes skills take time to learn. If they learn to sit quietly with God's Word in a group, they will become much more comfortable sitting with the Word on their own. Remind them that spending time in the Bible each day is one of the most valuable things they can do as believers in Christ.

PREPARATION

It's not necessary for group members to prepare anything for the study ahead of time. However, at the end of each study are five days' worth of suggestions for spending time in God's Word during the next week. These daily times are optional but valuable, so encourage the group to do them. Also, invite them to bring their questions and insights to the group at your next meeting, especially if they had a breakthrough moment or if they didn't understand something.

As the leader, there are a few things you should do to prepare for each meeting:

- *Read through the session.* This will help you become familiar with the content and know how to structure the discussion times.

- *Spend five to ten minutes doing the* Study It *questions on your own.* When the group meets, you'll be watching the clock, so you'll probably have a more fulfilling time with the passage if you do the exercise ahead of time. You can then spend time in the passage again with the group. This way, you'll be sure to have the key verses for that session deeply in your mind.

- *Pray for your group.* Pray especially that God will guide them into a deeper understanding of how they can be thankful to Him in every area of life.

- *Bring extra supplies to your meeting.* Group members should bring their own pens for writing notes on the Bible reflection, but it is a good idea to have extras available for those who forget. You may also want to bring paper and Bibles for those who may have neglected to bring their study guides to the meeting.

Below you will find suggested answers for some of the study questions. Note that in many cases there is no one right answer, especially when group members are sharing their personal experiences.

Session 1: Giving Thanks for God's Abundance

1. *Answers will vary. The goal here is to get people thinking about thankfulness and opening up to each other about the topic of being grateful to God.*

2. *Some people have a harder time noticing good things than others do. It's less a matter of how much hardship a person has in his or her life than it is a matter of attitude. Some people are naturally more attuned to negative input than positive input. The goal of this whole study is to help each person in the group make progress in noticing and responding to things for which he or she can be grateful.*

3. *Eve focused on the one fruit she couldn't have rather than being thankful for the many good things that God had made freely available to her. This negative focus darkened her mind, and she succumbed to the temptation to eat the forbidden fruit.*

4. *When we focus on what we don't have or on what we're displeased about, our minds become "darkened" like Eve's. We take for granted the countless gifts of God. We look for what is wrong and refuse to enjoy life until the negative things are "fixed." We're also more likely to resent God and try to get our own way because we see Him as stingy.*

5. *If we acknowledge the fact that all we have and all we are belong to God, we are more likely to see our need to be truly grateful to Him for allowing us to use and enjoy the resources He has provided. On the other hand, if we think those things belong to us, we're less likely to see them as gifts to be thankful for.*

6. *God could look at what we currently rely on as a gift He has graciously bestowed on us, not as something we've earned. Where He has provided for us generously, we may worry that we won't have enough.*

7. *Satan promised that if Eve ate the fruit, she would be like God, knowing good and evil. However, when she and Adam actually ate the fruit, they only felt shame and wanted to cover themselves. In addition, Satan said Adam and Eve wouldn't die if they ate the fruit, but they did die spiritually the moment they sinned—and the process was begun that would lead eventually to their physical deaths.*

8. *Eve could have thought something like this: God has provided abundantly for my need for food. I am so grateful for His provision and for the privilege of being intimate with Him that I will obey His command about this one tree, even though I don't understand the reason for it. This fruit is appealing, but the Lord has given me life, He has given me Adam, and He has given me this beautiful garden. I can trust Him to provide for me in all ways and be sure that He will withhold nothing good.*

9. *Among the many possibilities, some examples could include physical pain, not enough money, a job we don't like, or a relationship we don't have.*

10. *Answers will vary. It's fine for this process to be unfamiliar to the group members at first. Be sure to keep track of time.*

11. *Answers will vary.*

12. *Answers will vary. Note that some people may find the silence intimidating initially. Their anxiety might tempt them to fill the air with noise, but it will be helpful for these group members to just take a quiet moment before God. Let them express their discomfort once you're all gathered together again, but make sure it is balanced by those who found the silence strengthening. Helping people become comfortable with this "holy quiet" will serve their private daily times with God in wonderful ways.*

13. *Take as much time as you can to pray for each other. You might have someone write down the requests so you can keep track of answers to prayer.*

Session 2: Giving Thanks for God's Provision

1. *Some examples could include feeling we don't have all the things our friends or neighbors have; wishing our lives looked more like the other "perfect" families we know; or acting out on these feelings by grumbling, complaining, or being rude to others.*

2. *Answers will vary, but most likely, feelings of self-pity will come when we compare ourselves to others and decide we don't measure up, when we feel we are being treated unfairly, or when some trial hits and we can't understand why we have to go through it.*

3. *Self-pity is like a pit with crumbling edges: once we start feeling sorry for ourselves, we slide deeper and deeper into this negative hole—and it's harder and harder to climb back out into a place of contentment. When Christians get stuck in self-pity, it ultimately saps our relationship with God and with other people, leaving us feeling isolated.*

4. *When we are thankful to God, we focus on the good things that are happening. These things loom larger in our eyes, and what we lack appears smaller. Thankfulness to God opens us to His Presence, which offers protection from many negative states, including self-pity.*

5. *When we grumble, we are basically saying the world isn't going the way it should—according to us. This challenges God's role as the Sovereign of the universe. It's okay to feel sadness when life doesn't follow our plan, but grumbling goes beyond disappointment to actively challenging God's design and infinite knowledge. It also causes us to doubt God's provision in our lives.*

6. *When the people of God perceive life through a grid of gratitude, we can look at a difficult day at work, for example, and say, "Thank You, Jesus, for providing me with the strength to handle these challenges, just as You've provided a way through these kinds of obstacles in the past." We literally see the situation as manageable because we are viewing it with different eyes.*

7. *The Israelites now remembered Egypt as a place where they ate as much as they wanted, including meat. It's possible they did eat meat in Egypt, but as slaves they were more likely to eat mostly bread—and not necessarily all they wanted. They were glamorizing the past while conveniently forgetting the* *suffering they had faced and how much they had complained to God about their plight at the time.*

8. *Answers will vary. Try to think of something in your own life that you're tempted to complain about, and be ready to share it with the group if others are slow to answer.*

9. *The Lord gave the people quail one evening, and after that He gave them manna every day—though just enough for that day. The people didn't have extra, but they did have enough for their needs. Some in the group may be able to list numerous ways the Lord has provided for them, while others may have trouble thanking Him for His provision. Hopefully, as people vent their feelings in these discussion times, they will become aware of their attitudes that need adjustment!*

10. *Some group members may say yes, it would be easier, because the provision would so obviously be from God and not from their own hard labor. Others may say no, it wouldn't be easier, because getting the same manna day after day would get boring—and sinful hearts would be tempted to grumble about it. The key is that grumbling is in the heart of the grumbler, and he or she will find something to complain about no matter the situation.*

11. *Answers will vary.*

12. *Answers will vary.*

13. *Responses will vary.*

Session 3: Giving Thanks for Rescue

1. *As group members respond, take note of those who rate their lives at a 1 or 2, and plan to pray for them at the end of your meeting.*

2. *It is certainly more difficult to be thankful when we rate our lives more toward "agonizingly hard" than "absolutely fabulous." However, even in seasons of adversity, there is always something for which we can be thankful.*

3. *Whereas questions 1 and 2 asked about life in general, this one drills down specifically to your group members' lives today. If they can be thankful for this day, even with all its flaws, they are making progress. Still, your meetings should be a safe place for people to admit their tendency toward resentment, because they can't grow if they feel they have to hide the truth.*

4. *Focusing on adversity actually hinders our awareness of God's Presence, while focusing on thankfulness magnifies His work in our lives. As we make the choice to be thankful, it kick-starts this upward cycle.*

5. *Answers will vary. One example of "scales" falling from our eyes might include seeing a situation in a new light, discovering how God really was there with us in a situation, and understanding the riches He provided to us at that time. Gratitude always plays a part in this process because it allows us to focus on something other than ourselves and our own problems—which in turn allows us to see the situation from a different perspective.*

6. *When we lead a life of praise and thankfulness, it opens our eyes to the miracles God is doing around us every day that we might have previously overlooked. We are more likely to make positive choices, treat others with love and kindness, and look for ways to bless them—which will lead to having healthier relationships. A life of praise and thankfulness also positions us to receive other blessings from God, even healings and restorations. God doesn't guarantee everything will go our way if we are thankful, but we will more readily expect good things to happen.*

7. *Psalm 107:4–9 describes the homeless getting homes and being rescued from hunger and thirst. Verses 10–16 speak of prisoners doing hard labor being set free. Verses 17–22 describe people who became sick because of their sin, and* *when they turned back to God, He healed them. Verses 23–32 speak of rescue from shipwreck at sea.*

8. *Answers will vary, but you might want to have the group share some stories of rescue to encourage one another. The Lord doesn't always make everything instantly better, as the end of this psalm makes clear. Sometimes He allows our suffering to last much longer than we wish, and sometimes He allows tragedies to happen that will never be fixed in this life. But He often rescues us in our difficulties—and He is ever faithful to save His followers eternally.*

9. *We build this habit so that the next time we face hardship we have a strong memory of God's unfailing love. This memory will help to carry us through the new hard place. When things aren't going well, it's easy for negative feelings to fill our consciousness, and a list of rescues to rehearse can counteract this.*

10. *Allow group members to briefly tell their stories of redemption from sin or from some experience of suffering. It is important for each of us to call to mind these narratives because they reinforce our gratitude and motivate others to think of their own redemption stories. Those who hear our "good reports" will also be more likely to recognize God's love and kindness in their particular situations and realize their need to be thankful. Sharing these stories helps others know us better too, which strengthens the bonds of friendship.*

11. *Answers will vary.*

12. *Answers will vary.*

13. *Responses will vary.*

Session 4: Giving Thanks for Trials

1. *Allow a few minutes for the group members to share their trials.*

2. *Answers will vary.*

3. *Every problem we face can either help transform us into the masterpiece God intended or become a stumbling block that hinders us. When we "make friends" with our problems, we see them in a different light, recognizing that God is truly in control of all that happens. Rather than striving to fix everything ourselves, we rely on the power of God—and this teaches us to trust in Him.*

4. *Once again, make your group a safe place for people to admit their struggles. Encourage them to consider what "defiance" looks like in their lives (complaining, anger, bargaining). While it may take time for them to get to the point of trusting God on any given issue, it's good for them to be aware of where they are in the process.*

5. *As soon as we become aware that our minds are chewing on a difficulty, we should go to God in prayer and thank Him for His promise to never leave us on our own during a time of trial (see Hebrews 13:5). We should also express our thankfulness as He reveals the ways He has already been working on our behalf, as He shows us the course to take to handle the situation, and as He brings us to a place of resolution. The thanksgiving must always come first, because this affects how our minds respond to the difficulty and how receptive we are to God's guidance.*

6. *Answers will vary. For many of the challenges we face, some advance planning is needed—the reading is not intended to encourage procrastination—but it's important for us not to worry about the things we cannot solve ahead of time. If we do find ourselves borrowing problems from tomorrow, we should acknowledge that things* **are** *out of our control and leave those issues in God's hands. This readies us to get to work when God calls us to step back into the situation and take action.*

7. *James says we should rejoice when we face trials because having our faith tested leads to perseverance—which is the habit of continuing to work at something even when it is hard. Perseverance, in turn, is a key component of* *spiritual maturity. We will struggle to thank God for our trials until we develop a habit of doing so in the midst of suffering.*

8. *Paul agrees with James that we should rejoice in God always, including when we face trials. He says we should respond to trials not with rage but with gentleness, which, according to Scripture, is a position of strength, not weakness. This means choosing not to retaliate, even when we could do so.*

9. *Thanksgiving is an important part of our response to trials because it leads us to involve God in the process and recognize He is in control. A response without thanksgiving would be heavy with desperate requests for God to rescue us from the trial. There would be a thread of anxiety running through our prayers, making it harder for us to pray in faith. Thanksgiving is crucial for "cleaning out" the faithless anxiety from our prayers.*

10. *God's Peace becomes part of every believer's real-life experience when he or she prays with thanksgiving and thereby chooses not to give in to feelings of anxiety.*

11. *Answers will vary.*

12. *Answers will vary.*

13. *Responses will vary.*

Session 5: Giving Thanks for Spiritual Blessings

1. *Answers will vary, but every person who has repented of their sins and accepted God's gift of salvation can certainly claim the blessings of knowing their sins are forgiven and having a place reserved for them in heaven (see John 14:2–3).*

2. *While there won't be time for people to tell their entire testimony, they can tell how old they were when they became aware of God's mercy and share a few of the circumstances surrounding their coming to faith in Christ.*

3. *When we lead a life of thankfulness, we walk purposefully through the day, allowing God to direct our course one step at a time, grateful along the way for His provision. Thankfulness says that all things—whether they seem good or bad—come from the hand of a loving and sovereign God.*

4. *Instead of choosing to pay attention to the negative things that happen to us, a grateful heart chooses instead to pay attention to the positives. Negative things simply don't register as strongly, and our mood isn't as affected by them. We don't drift into negative thought patterns where we're imagining the worst-case scenarios over and over but instead remain in a state where we are trusting in God for the outcome.*

5. *Thanking God in every situation helps us develop the habit of praying without ceasing, which Paul urges in 1 Thessalonians 5:16–18. Thanking God also crowds out our worrying and complaining. It is impossible to think anxious thoughts and thankful thoughts at the same time.*

6. *Answers will vary but could include patterns such as habitual worry, complaining, impulsiveness, selfishness, or self-criticism.*

7. *Some examples of answers could include, "I'm thankful for being adopted into God's family, because I long for the sense that I belong to someone." Or, "I'm thankful for God's grace, because I know that I make mistakes, and I need His help every day." Or, "I'm grateful for the Holy Spirit living inside of me, because I really do want to live a holy life, and without Him empowering me, I would never manage it." Paul urges us to not overlook these spiritual blessings because it is important for us to recognize the price that Jesus paid to provide them. As believers, we have been made new in Christ! This is the root of our thankfulness.*

8. *Some of the things we learn about God's nature from Ephesians 1:3–14 include: He chooses us as His children before we choose Him, He wants us to be in His family, He lavishes His grace on us, He is generous, He is self-sacrificing, and He is sovereign over everything that happens.*

9. *All of the blessings God showers on us as His children come to us because we are "in Christ." We are not left on our own to deal with the world. Rather, we are joined to Christ and can have a moment-by-moment awareness of His Presence with us.*

10. *These concepts can become more real to us if we take the time to reflect on them. We can focus on just one word—***chosen***—and mull it over until it sinks deep into our hearts. Or we can talk about these ideas with another person until we get it. Journaling is another way to absorb these blessings into our hearts.*

11. *Answers will vary.*

12. *Answers will vary.*

13. *Responses will vary.*

Session 6: Giving Thanks for the Cross

1. *This is an "icebreaker" question, so the main goal is for group members to get to know each other better. But it is also worth being aware that if we first heard about the cross as children, the radical, shocking aspect of it may not come as vividly to mind now. That's why it's important to take a fresh look at the cross so that it strikes us once more as an amazing thing for Christ to do on our behalf.*

2. *Some in the group may have accepted Christ at an early age with few questions. Others might have struggled with giving up the control of their lives, or with questioning if God would really do this for them, or with other doubts or struggles—and one or two may not yet have made this decision. Encourage the group members to take a fresh look at their journey.*

3. *Out of everything Jesus has done, going to the cross displays His love most vividly to us. If our own suffering tempts us to doubt His love, His suffering will overcome those doubts. Jesus voluntarily endured unimaginable torture and* punishment—that He didn't deserve and that He could have escaped—because He loved us so much.

4. Answers will vary. Help your group be a safe place for people to admit if they have trouble keeping Jesus' love in mind when they go through hard times. It's one thing to believe in His love in our heads and another thing to have it saturate our being so that it fuels our response to every event.

5. Jesus won't fall off His throne if we "shake our fist" and rage at Him, but doing so isn't good for us. We can easily get stuck in self-pity if we go that way. It's much better to confess our anger to God and ask for His help in learning to thank Him in the midst of our suffering.

6. Thankfulness makes us aware of God's Presence, and His Presence makes our problems seem smaller and more manageable. It also develops our faith in God as we trust in His goodness in the midst of the difficulty. Of course, being thankful in this way doesn't come easily, which is why we need to persist in practicing it until it shapes our hearts.

7. Jesus refused the gall because He purposefully chose to experience the full extent of the suffering that was ordained for Him. He wasn't looking for a shortcut; He was undergoing this torture for a reason: to pay the penalty for our sins.

8. As the Son of God, Jesus indeed could have come down from the cross or commanded angels to free Him. He was no helpless victim, but a willing victim. That didn't lessen His terrible suffering; in fact, it made His suffering even more astonishing. Who among us would willingly undergo such agony for others?

9. Answers will vary. Only by reflecting deeply on what Jesus really went through can our hearts be pierced by His love and can we express our thankfulness for what He willingly endured.

10. *Paul writes that "God made him who had no sin to be sin for us, so that in him we might become the righteousness of God" (2 Corinthians 5:21). Jesus took on Himself all of our sins and suffered the just penalty for them so those who believe in Him would be spared from that penalty. His act made it possible for sinners like us to have peace with God and enjoy His Presence. This is why we should be thankful to Jesus for what He has done!*

11. *Answers will vary.*

12. *Answers will vary.*

13. *Responses will vary.*

Session 7: Giving Thanks for the Resurrection

1. *Later in the session, the group will look at the apostle Paul's answer to this question in 1 Corinthians 15:17–19. But for now, allow the group members to express their ideas and opinions on the importance of Jesus' resurrection.*

2. *Answers will vary. Some Christians regard every Sunday as Easter, so they are continually celebrating Jesus' resurrection and the new life they have been given.*

3. *Without gratitude, we tend to be suspicious toward Jesus, essentially asking, "What have You done for me lately?" while failing to clearly see the abundant answers to that question. We view Him through the distorted lens of our insatiable wants, which blocks our view of His beauty and goodness and trustworthiness. All these things get stripped away when we practice gratitude.*

4. *Some of us just seem to be born with a greater need to feel in charge of our worlds. Others among us felt powerless in our chaotic childhoods, so we crave control as adults. In either case, this ingrained habit needs to be overwritten with a new habit of yielding control to Jesus. We can build that habit by*

letting go of control in smaller areas and working our way up to bigger things.
The Holy Spirit will help us in this process if we ask Him to do so.

5. *If we are convinced that God is good, it changes our outlook on the*
struggles we are facing. As believers in Christ, we will be secure in the
knowledge that He will not let anything ultimately—eternally—harm us, even
if we or our loved ones die. Those tragedies can still be woven into a tapestry
of God's goodness, because death is not the final word in any believer's story.
Beyond death there is resurrection. If we're convinced of that fact, then
nothing in this life can threaten our well-being.

6. *The Bible depicts Jesus as totally trustworthy. Christ said that He would*
die and rise again—and He did die and rise again. The resurrection is
evidence that God does what He says. He allowed His followers to suffer in
order to demonstrate the strength of their faith to themselves and to outsiders;
yet even when they died, He was with them (see Acts 7:54–60). If we doubt the
trustworthiness of Jesus, we can read the Gospels and the book of Acts to see
how He persistently cared for people and how He did what He promised—and
still does today. In addition, the entire history of the church tells of men and
women who trusted in Jesus and experienced His Presence no matter what
they went through.

7. *Death is the penalty of sin. In dying, Christ paid the penalty for all who*
confess Him as Lord and Savior. In rising, He showed that He was greater
than death. So if Christ was not raised, then death—the penalty for sin—has
not been conquered and His death could not provide forgiveness of our sins.
As Paul states in Romans 4:25, "He was delivered over to death for our sins
and was raised to life for our justification."

8. *In popular imagination, heaven is a place where disembodied people float*
around, play harps, sing endless (and not very interesting) songs, and don't
do much else. However, with resurrected bodies, we look forward to doing
all kinds of creative activity in a new Earth full of the beauties of nature

unravaged by sin. Our bodies will be strong, whole, and immortal. We will feast together and enjoy the wonder of God's Presence intimately.

9. *Paul put up with persistent pain during his traveling ministry to spread the gospel. He was arrested, beaten, robbed, shipwrecked, and endured many other sufferings (see 2 Corinthians 11:23–27). He endured all this because of his hope of eternal reward. The people to whom he preached likewise suffered persecution for their faith. They too endured injustice because of their faith and looked forward to the ultimate justice they would receive in the next life. If that hope was empty, their lives were pitiable. All Christians' sufferings are likewise endurable because they expect that God will heal everything in eternity.*

10. *"Fallen asleep" is a figure of speech referring to death. Those who have died with faith in Christ are not dead and gone but are with Christ now, waiting to be clothed again in resurrected bodies like His. Jesus' resurrection was the "firstfruits," or first portion, of a harvest to come: the resurrection of His followers. Jesus' resurrection is the evidence and guarantee that ours is coming. It guarantees that, for those of us who are believers, our sins really are forgiven and that resurrection and an abundant, wondrous future in heaven, reunited with loved ones who died as followers of Christ, really is our destiny. Contemplating what is in store for us should make us persistently joyful, regardless of our present circumstances.*

11. *Answers will vary.*

12. *Answers will vary.*

13. *Responses will vary.*

Session 8: Giving Thanks for the Holy Spirit

1. *Some common misperceptions about the Holy Spirit include: He first appeared on the Day of Pentecost (when the believers spoke in tongues); He is* *only active in certain places; He only does spectacular or miraculous acts; He only dwells in "super spiritual" Christians.*

2. *Allow the group members some time to describe how they see (or fail to see) the Holy Spirit at work in their lives. If necessary, clarify the difference between "intuition" (the ability we all have to instinctively understand things in our situation) and the knowledge that comes to believers through the work of the Holy Spirit, which is a supernatural form of wisdom that goes beyond their own human capacities for reason.*

3. *Thankfulness lowers our emotional and spiritual walls, making us more relaxed and transparent. We're less resistant to the Holy Spirit and more open to His action in and through us. We're also less preoccupied and more available to hear what the Holy Spirit might be saying to us.*

4. *Many of us get stuck in the negative—it's not at all rare. Hopefully, by practicing thankfulness throughout this study, you and your group members are building a better habit. When we get stuck in the negative, we need to resist those thoughts, take them captive, and make them obedient to Christ (see 2 Corinthians 10:5). Gratitude to God helps us focus on Him and break away from these negative thought patterns.*

5. *God's sovereignty is His kingship and authority over everything. Because He is sovereign, He controls the whole cosmos. We thank God in all circumstances because, as sovereign, He has expressly allowed all circumstances and is at work in all circumstances.*

6. *Complaining says that God isn't good enough, wise enough, or powerful enough to run the universe—or even our lives. It challenges His goodness, His wisdom, and His power, and it concludes that painful events in our lives must be bad events allowed by a bad God. Then again, sometimes in our complaints, we don't think about God's sovereignty at all; we forget that He* has the power and authority to orchestrate every single thing that happens. Typically though, whether we realize it or not, our complaint is deliberately directed at God's sovereignty, questioning why an all-powerful God would allow this tragedy to happen.

7. Truly loving Jesus leads naturally to doing what He commands. In John 13:34, Christ gave this command: "Love one another. As I have loved you, so you must love one another." The Holy Spirit fills us and empowers us when we are committed to loving Jesus and one another.

8. The Holy Spirit testifies to the truth and equips us to testify, like a legal advocate in court. He comes alongside us as believers in Christ and helps us to do what we can't do in our own resources alone. He guides us to know and understand truth—both the true things that Jesus has taught His followers, and other things we need to know.

9. Answers will vary. A person's experiences and church background tend to define how he or she expects the Holy Spirit to work. Some Christians may not expect to feel His promptings. They may not ask Him to fill and empower them because they don't believe He is active in that way.

10. Answers will vary. In the book of Acts, we read how the Holy Spirit empowered the early believers to speak God's word with conviction and take bold acts of faith—which will seem attractive to some but possibly a bit frightening to others. Acknowledge any doubts your group members might have and encourage them to take their concerns to God in prayer.

11. Answers will vary.

12. Answers will vary.

13. Responses will vary.

Also Available in the
Jesus Calling® Bible Study Series

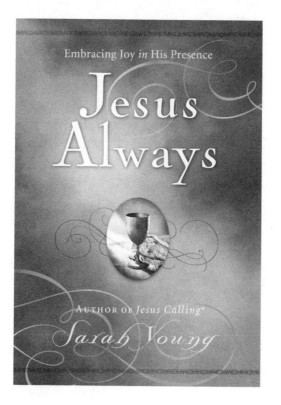

If you liked reading this book, you may enjoy these other titles by *Sarah Young*

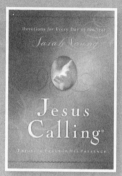

Jesus Calling®
Hardcover

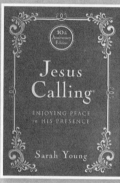

Jesus Calling® 10th Anniversary Edition
Bonded Leather

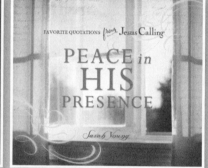

Peace in His Presence:
Favorite Quotations from Jesus Calling®
Padded Hardcover

Jesus Calling® for Kids
Hardcover

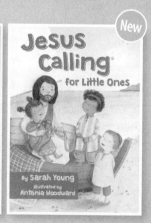

Jesus Calling® Bible Storybook
Hardcover

Jesus Calling® for Little Ones
Board Book